Flavorsome F Crepe Cookbook

A Detailed Cookbook Featuring Best 30 Crepe Recipes

BY: Ivy Hope

Copyright © 2020 by Ivy Hope

IVY HOPE
COOKBOOK

Copyright/License Page

Please don't reproduce this book. It means you are not allowed to make any type of copy (print or electronic), sell, publish, disseminate or distribute. Only people who have written permission from the author are allowed to do so.

This book is written by the author taking all precautions that the content is true and helpful. However, the reader needs to be careful about his/her action. If anything happens due to the reader's actions the author won't be taken as responsible.

Table of Contents

Introduction 5

1. Pumpkin Crepe with Beer 7

2. Fruit Salsa Crepe 10

3. Chicken Broccoli Crepe 13

4. Spinach Artichoke Crepe 17

5. Peach and Cream Crepe with Vanilla 20

6. Boston Crème Crepe 23

7. Dark Chocolate Crepe 27

8. Norwegian Potato Crepe 30

9. Blueberry Lemon Crepe 33

10. Lasagna Ricotta Crepe 36

11. Red Velvet Thin Crepe 39

12. Cinnamon Apple Crepe 42

13. Nutella Strawberry Crepe 45

14. Brown butter Crepe with Bananas 48

15. Lemon Crepe 51

16. Black Forest Crepe 54

17. Oreo Beer Crepe 57

18. Poppyseed Lemon Crepe with Blueberry Cream Filling 60

19. Orange Crepe 64

20. Mix Vegetable Crepe 67

21. Chicken and Mushroom Crepe 70

22. Apple Walnut Crepe 73

23. Buckwheat Mushroom Savory Galette 76

24. Shrimp Florentine Crepe 79

25. Chocolate Strawberry Crepe 82

26. Lemon Strawberry Crepe 85

27. Vanilla Apple with Beer Crepe 88

28. Lobster Newburg Crepe 91

29. Grape Cream Crepe 94

30. Avocado Crepe 97

Conclusion 100

About the Author 101

Author's Afterthoughts 102

Introduction

Do you love treating yourself with delicious desserts? Do you need help with improving your cooking skills? Do you want to start your food blog and get into fame? If the answer to all the questions is yes, then this is the right book that you have picked from your collection. Crepes are loved by everyone, right from teens to grandparents to friends, everyone is attached to a deliciously flavored crepe. Crepes are commonly considered as pancakes but thinner and subtle. They have a long history coming from the grounds of France.

Crepes are easy to prepare recipes and have a tendency to save your time. Gone are the days when baking was considered the most tricky task. Thanks to this amazing free cookbook, which will provide you with the best crepe recipes in the world. Even if you are new to the basics of cooking and baking crepes, this cookbook will solve every problem.

The process of filling creeps using hot orange sauce mixed with chilled beer is mouth-watering. Discover ways in which you can improve your creativity while preparing delicious crepes. Without any further ado, let's get into the scrumptious world of crepes.

1. Pumpkin Crepe with Beer

Pumpkin crepes are dipped in chilled beer to enhance its raw flavors. French bakers are more profound for their sweet tooth audience. The juicy pumpkin melts its flavor after dipping it in the beer pound. You can garnish the crepe with apple cinnamon and curry leaves. It tastes heaven when frosted with royal cream and honey. They can be treated as usual pan desserts on various occasions.

Ingredients

- 2 eggs
- ¼ tsp. ginger
- 3 tbsp. butter
- 1 juicy apple
- ½ cup blended pumpkin puree
- 2 cups toned milk
- 1 (5.3 oz) divine milk
- Chocolate bar
- Baking powder
- ¼ cup brown sugar
- ½ tbsp. cinnamon
- 1-2 cup flour
- ¼ nutmeg
- Salt (acc.to taste)
- 1 tbsp. vanilla essence
- 1 tbsp. Refined sugar
- ½ cup pumpkin ale

Serving size: 3 crepes

Cooking time: 45 minutes

Instructions

1. Melt the butter in a hot saucepan.

2. Add milk to the same saucepan and keep it for 10 min till the butter melts properly.

3. While the milk and butter are boiling, whisk the eggs, vanilla, and pumpkin together.

4. Pour the milk in the pumpkin mix slowly and stir.

5. Mix together flour, sugar, baking powder, salt, cinnamon, ginger and nutmeg in a separate bowl.

6. Pour this dry material into wet material.

7. Whisk it till the mixture becomes smooth.

8. Pour 1/3 of this batter at a time on a crepe maker or stove to prepare the crepe.

9. After the preparation of crepes, prepare the fillings.

10. In a saucepan, sauté the butter, apple, brown sugar, pumpkin ale, cinnamon.

11. Simmer it on low heat until the pumpkin ale becomes a thick sauce.

12. Melt the chocolate bar safely.

13. Fold the crepe into quarters and serve with the fillings and melted chocolate.

2. Fruit Salsa Crepe

The aroma of delicious sautéed fruits with salsa sauce will not let you live easily. You will crave for the fruit salsa crepe every minute. It is the combination of juicy fruits and berries topped with salsa sauce. An impeccable Sunday brunch to lower down your hunger starts with this delicious salsa crepe. Hence, no more mercy to your Belly! Huh! It is very nutritious and healthy with lots of powerful effects of vitamin A, proteins, etc.

Ingredients

- 2 chopped Apple
- 1 pint of strawberries (may also choose other berries)
- 2 kiwis
- 2/3 mussel man's Apple butter
- 2 fresh peaches
- 1 cup flour
- 2 eggs
- ½ cup baking soda
- 2 tbsp. sugar
- ½ tbsp. vanilla
- Pinch of salt
- ½ cup club soda
- Whipped cream
- Caramel sauce

Serving size: 3 crepes

Cooking time: 45 minutes

Instructions

1. Sauté all the fruits in a bowl and keep it aside.

2. Add Mussulmen's apple butter on sautéed fruits.

3. Keep this mixture in the fridge for 1 hour.

4. Mix flour, eggs, club soda, sugar, vanilla, salt and the baking powder in a mixture and

5. Mix it well.

6. Freeze the crepe batter for 30 minutes.

7. Preheat the saucepan in low flame and spray the cooking spray over it.

8. Pour ¼ cup of crepe batter in the saucepan at a time.

9. Spread the batter properly all over the pan by tilting the pan slowly.

10. Keep the batter until it becomes golden brown in between and crispy from the edge

11. Turn the crepe over.

12. Continue cooking until it becomes golden brown from either side.

13. Remove the crepe from the pan. Fold it in the half and place it on a plate.

14. Top it with fruit salsa. Fill the crepe with it.

15. Fold the crepe again and top it with caramel sauce and whipped cream.

3. Chicken Broccoli Crepe

Chicken broccoli crepe is loaded with cheese sauce and crispy green broccoli. Broccoli is famous for its high protein contents, making it suitable for gym freaks. The thick marinated sauce brings out the tasty side of the crepe. Chicken is kept marinated in the aromatic red sauce to flavor it up. Meanwhile, the boiling broccoli provides intense color to the crepe. Mostly, the chicken broccoli crepe is considered for dinner in many french families.

Ingredients

For crepe:

- 2 cups of milk
- 3 eggs
- 2tsp salt
- 1 cup flour
- 3 tbsp. melted butter

For filling and sauce:

- 3 ½ chicken breasts (chopped cubed shaped)
- 1 tbsp olive oil
- ¼ tsp. salt
- 4 tsp pepper and onion powder
- 3 tbsp butter
- 6 tbsp flour
- ½ cup sliced almonds (optional)
- 3 cups fresh chopped and boiled broccoli
- ¾ grated cheddar cheese
- ¼ tsp. pepper
- 2 cups of milk
- ½ tsp. Salt

Serving size: 4 crepes

Cooking time: 25 minutes

Instructions

1. Mix all the ingredients required for a crepe in a blender till it becomes smooth.

2. Chill for 30-45 minutes to thicken.

3. In a non-stick pan, pour 3 tbsp. of crepe batter. Swirl the pan in a clockwise direction to spread the batter equally over the pan.

4. In medium heat, cook the batter until it becomes thin.

5. Flip it to the other side. Cook for 2-3 minutes until it becomes brown-red in Color.

6. Cook all crepes and keep aside.

7. Pour 2tbsp olive oil in a preheat non-stick pan and add chicken cubes to it.

8. Remove chicken and set aside.

9. In the same pan, melt 3tbsp of butter. Pour flour and milk slowly together. Whisk till thick.

10. Boil for at least 5 minutes to remove the flour smell.

11. Add salt, cheese, and pepper.

12. Mix well. Set aside about half a cup of sauce for dressing.

13. In the remaining sauce, add boiled chicken and broccoli.

14. Stir till marinated. Remove from heat.

15. Fill all the crepes with chicken broccoli mix. Place into two greased 9 x 13-inch pans. Cover with foil and bake at 350°F for 15 to 20 minutes, or till hot.

16. Pour the sauce that was kept aside.

17. Garnish with sliced almonds if needed.

4. Spinach Artichoke Crepe

Spinach is famous for its juicy green leaves and marinating flavor. It's even considered helpful to boost up your immune system. On the other hand, artichoke comes with a truck full of nutrients. Spinach and artichoke crepe is a super versatile formula for health boost up and fresh eating. You can easily prepare this recipe at home within half an hour. It is easy to make and is delicious. Spinach and artichoke is the best combination used for filling crepes.

Ingredients

- 2 fresh farm spinach
- 1 cup all-purpose flour
- 2 cup flour
- 1 ½ tsp. salt
- 3 eggs
- 1 1/3 cup milk
- 2 cup frozen artichokes, chopped
- 3 cloves garlic
- 2 tsp. olive oil
- 2 tbsp. low-fat cream cheese
- 2 cup Greek yogurt
- Salt and pepper
- 1/4 cup cheese
- 1 cup mozzarella cheese

Serving size: 4 crepes

Cooking time: 45 minutes

Instructions:

1. In a big bowl, mix flour and salt together and mix it with your hands.

2. Add eggs in the same bowl. Mix egg and flour while pouring milk slowly in the bowl.

3. Whisk till the batter becomes smooth.

4. Leave it for 5-10 minutes.

5. Preheat the non-stick pan in medium-high flame.

6. Add ¼ of batter that is previously prepared on the pan and swirl it until the batter spreads properly all over the pan.

7. Let the edges cook properly. Flip around to cook it from the other side as well.

8. Continue cooking until the color of crepe changes to brownish red.

9. Once cooked, transfer the crepe to a plate and keep it aside.

10. In another non-stick pan pour 1 tbsp. of olive oil. Add 3 garlic cloves and sauté for 40 seconds.

11. Add spinach and farm artichoke. Cook them properly.

12. Remove the pan and mix it with cheese and cream. Add some salt and pepper according to taste.

13. Sauté the filling properly. Fill each crepe with the spinach artichoke filling and serve with hot tomato sauce (optional).

5. Peach and Cream Crepe with Vanilla

It might take several attempts, but you will not regret learning this recipe. Peach and cream crepe are salivating and more tempting once filled with vanilla. The lush lucid color of peaches pops up brightly once cooked with sautéed cream. No wonder why this crepe is most famous amongst all. It is sweet and smooth with all the flavors mixed properly. You should put your hands on this special piece.

Ingredients

- 1 cup all-purpose flour
- 2 cup flour
- 1 ½ tsp. salt
- 3 eggs
- 1 1/3 cup milk
- 5 tbsp. unsalted melted butter
- 4 peaches. Chopped
- 2 tbsp. Lemon juice
- 2 tbsp. olive oil
- 2 Tbsp. heavy cream
- ½ cup mascarpone cheese for garnishing

Serving size: 3 crepes

Cooking time: 45 minutes

Instructions:

1. Blend the flour, milk, eggs, 2 tbsp. butter in the blender properly.

2. Add 1 tbsp. of raw sugar and ½ tbsp. salts to the mixture.

3. Make the batter smooth.

4. In a bowl, combine chopped peaches, lemon juice, and sugar.

5. Sauté till the peaches properly combine with lemon juice.

6. Leave it for 30 minutes. (Peach releases some juice which is normal.)

7. Preheat the non-stick pan at the medium-low flame. Pour 1 cup of batter to the pan and swirl the pan to distribute the batter evenly.

8. Cook for 5-6 minutes and flip the other side after that.

9. Continue cooking till the color of the crepe changes to a golden brown.

10. Transfer the crepe to the plate.

11. Preheat the oven to 400F. Place 1/8 of the peach in each of the crepes separately.

12. Take a baking sheet and brush it with some butter using a fork.

13. Fold the crepe in a triangle shape and add ½ peaches again.

14. Bake till it becomes hot. Put them on a baking sheet. Brush the top of the crepe with granulated sugar and butter.

15. Add 1 scoop of vanilla ice cream over the top of the crepe. (optional)

16. Serve with mascarpone cream.

6. Boston Crème Crepe

You will definitely become obsessed with Boston cream crepe. As the name suggests, Once gone inside your mouth, it melts like a soft candy and tastes chocolatey. However, you can revive its crisp by adding raw sugar crunch over it. Every crepe is loaded with creamy and fluffy chocolate sauce to give your taste a new dimension. The recipe is very easy, and you can prepare it in your home. It is the perfect lunch theme for you and your family.

Ingredients

For crepe batter:

- 1 cup all-purpose flour
- 2 cup flour
- 1 ½ tsp. salt
- 3 eggs
- 1 1/3 cup milk
- 5 tbsp. unsalted melted butter

For fillings:

- 1 cup of sugar
- 2 cup corn-starch
- 1/2 tsp. salt
- 1 1/2 cups milk
- 4 egg whites
- 1 tsp. vanilla extract
- 2 cup whipping cream

Serving size: 3 crepes

Cooking time: 1 hour

Instructions

1. Mix flour, eggs, club soda, sugar, vanilla, salt and the baking powder in a mixture and whisk it well.

2. Freeze the crepe batter for 30 minutes.

3. Preheat the saucepan in low flame and spray the cooking spray over it.

4. Pour ¼ cup of crepe batter in the saucepan at a time.

5. Spread the batter properly all over the pan by tilting the pan slowly.

6. Keep the batter until it becomes golden brown in between and crispy from the edges.

7. Turn the crepe over.

8. Continue cooking until it becomes golden brown from either side.

9. Remove the crepe from the pan. Fold it in the half and place it on a plate.

10. In another saucepan, pour milk, corn-starch, sugar, salt on low flame.

11. Stir till it gets thicken.

12. Put 1/3 of the sugar mixture to egg whites and stir. Heat for 1 minute.

13. Switch off the heat and remove the pan. Pour vanilla extract into the mixture.

14. Refrigerate the filling for 2 hours.

15. Add whipping cream until stiff peaks are generated.

16. Fill all the crepes with this filling and serve.

7. Dark Chocolate Crepe

These vegan and extremely healthy chocolate crepes are made from raw milk; cheese spelled flour and tempting dark chocolate. Dark chocolate chips are something that you will never regret eating. Dark chocolate crepe is the famous food from a famous supernatural series where vampires hog on this sweet crepe throughout the series. You will never get tired of eating them. They are best suited for light breakfast. Do give them a try.

Ingredients

- Ounce cream cheese
- 5tbsp heavy cream
- 2 packs dark chocolate, chopped and melted
- 3 eggs
- 2 cups of milk
- 2 cup flour
- 3tbsp butter, melted
- ½ tsp. Salt
- Whipped cream
- Berries

Serving size: 4 crepes

Cooking time: 1 hour

Instructions

1. In a bowl, mix cream cheese, heavy cream and chopped and melted dark chocolate.

2. Whisk until it thickens.

3. In a blender, add flour, milk, eggs, butter, and salt. Blend it till the batter becomes smooth.

4. Preheat the non-stick pan and pour ¼ cup of batter in the pan.

5. Swirl it around so the batter can spread properly.

6. Cook until the color changes to brown.

7. Flip it and continue cooking until the sides are perfectly cooked.

8. Let the crepes cool.

9. Fill each crepe with the dark chocolate filling

10. Serve with berries.

8. Norwegian Potato Crepe

With the delicacy of Norwegian creme and crisp of potato, this crepe is ideal for brunch. It has a very creamy and crispy taste with flavored fillings of potato. In Norway, this dish is also called Lefse. You cannot stop loving this thin crispy roll filled with tempting fillings. The whole idea of serving potatoes inside a thin roll may sound odd at first, but the process of giving fluffiness and softness to the potato filling is incredible.

Ingredients

- 1 cup all-purpose flour
- 2 cup flour
- 1 ½ tsp. salt
- 3 eggs
- 1 1/3 cup milk
- 5 tbsp. melted butter
- 2 cup Chopped potato
- 2 tbsp raw sugar
- ½ tsp cinnamon
- Nutella (optional)
- 2 cup heavy whipping cream

Serving size: 4 crepes

Cooking time: 1 hour 30 minutes

Instructions

1. In a large bowl take potatoes and cover them with water.

2. Without cleaning the skin of the potato, boil them for 30 minutes.

3. After this, remove them from heat and peel the skin off.

4. Mash them in a bowl. You can also use a food processor for mashing.

5. Add heavy cream, salt, flour, sugar, butter in mashed potatoes.

6. Mix it all together properly.

7. Prepare a 40 g of dough and roll it into a small ball shape.

8. Freeze it for 30 minutes

9. Take out the balls and using a rolling pin roll it out.

10. Use linen to cover the working surface so that balls do not stick to the surface.

11. Now, preheat the pan at a medium-low flame.

12. Cook for 2 minutes on one side.

13. Continue cooking until the color changes to reddish-brown.

14. Switch off the pan. Keep the crepe aside on a plate.

15. Serve with Nutella garnishing and whipped cream.

9. Blueberry Lemon Crepe

The lemon juice aroma of Blueberry is tempting. It gives a beautiful popping color to the crepe. On the other hand, the zest of lemon works like wonders. The combination of blueberry and lemon is incredible. When mixed, they give out the best crepes for the breakfast table. You should hands-down taste this crepe. It has a unique sour and sweet taste, which will melt your taste buds. The revolutionary crepe which is unique and delicious.

Ingredients

- 1 cup all-purpose flour
- 2 cup flour
- 1 ½ tsp. salt
- 3 eggs
- 1 1/3 cup milk
- 5 tbsp. melted butter
- 1 lemon zest
- 2 eggs
- ⅔ blueberry jam
- 1tbsp
- Custard sauce (optional) for garnishing

Serving size: 5 crepes

Cooking time: 1 hour

Instructions

1. In a bowl, whisk the flour, sugar, lemon zest and salt together.

2. In a small bowl, whisk the eggs, milk, and 1tbsp of melted butter properly.

3. Add the egg mixture in the flour bowl slowly. Keep whisking properly.

4. Preheat the non-stick pan. Lightly coat it with butter.

5. Pour about 4 spoons of batter and swirl the pan until the batter reaches the edge of the pan.

6. Cook for 2 minutes and flip to the other side.

7. Continue cooking till the batter changes to golden brown color.

8. Repeat the same with another batter.

9. In a small pan, heat the blueberry jam. Mix the lemon juice in it and set aside.

10. Fill the filling into each crepe separately.

11. Brush the crepe with some butter on top.

12. Pour custard sauce according to the taste over the crepe.

13. Serve with love.

10. Lasagna Ricotta Crepe

Crepes are tempting! The delicious stuffing inside them is fantastic. Especially when it comes down to lasagna crepe, you can never forget the flavors it contains. Lasagna crepe is filled with ricotta and spinach filling, which is healthy and tasty at the same time. You can even pour custard sauce or Nutella to enhance its flavors. Well, the best part - the batter can never upset you. The perfect fluffy batter turns out the best crepe in the world. When confused, do try these amazing lasagna crepes for lunch.

Ingredients

- 1 cup all-purpose flour
- 2 cup flour
- 1 ½ tsp. salt
- 3 eggs
- 1 1/3 cup milk
- 5 tbsp. unsalted melted butter
- 2tbsp olive oil
- 1 ½ pound freshly ricotta
- 2 eggs
- 2 cloves garlic
- 1 ½ pound fresh baby spinach
- ¼ tsp nutmeg
- Salt and pepper

Serving size: 5 crepes

Cooking time: 1 hour

Instructions

1. For preparing crepe, in a bowl, whisk 3 cups of water, flour, oil, and salt to form a thin batter.

2. Cover it and keep aside for at least 1 hour.

3. Heat a non-stick pan on medium-low heat.

4. Pour 2 cups of batter on the pan and swirl it till the batter reaches the edge of the pan.

5. Heat until the bottom is reddish-brown and flip it to the other side once done.

6. Continue cooking till the crepe is ready.

7. Pile it on the plate and set aside.

8. In a medium bowl, mix ricotta and egg.

9. In a non-stick pan, put some oil and add garlic.

10. Cook the garlic until it becomes fragrant.

11. Add the spinach and cook it until it becomes mild and liquid is absorbed.

12. Soak the spinach and chop.

13. Add spinach to the ricotta. Also add pepper, salt, and nutmeg.

14. For lasagna, spread ¼ cup of marinara sauce on the baking pan.

15. Spread crepes in one layer till the pan is filled.

16. Add the ricotta spinach mixture and 1 cup of marinara sauce.

17. Cover with another layer of crepe, ricotta, and sauce.

18. Now heat at 375-degree in an oven for 30 minutes.

19. Sprinkle some parmesan cheese on the plate and serve the lasagna spinach ricotta crepe.

11. Red Velvet Thin Crepe

The essence of red velvet makes this crepe fantastic and beautiful. It contains raw sugar and whipped cream, which creates a delicate taste. You can add this to your breakfast recipe and impress your friends and family.

You can easily prepare this recipe in your kitchen with simple **Ingredients** and equipment. It is quite sugary and stiff, but the filling is the ultimate beauty with red crystals. If you have never made any crepe before, this can be the best recipe to start from scratch.

Ingredients

- 1 cup all-purpose flour
- 2 cup flour
- 1 ½ tsp. salt
- 2 eggs
- 1 1/3 cup milk
- 5 tbsp. unsalted melted butter
- 2tbsp olive oil
- 2 tbsp sifted cocoa powder
- 2 cups buttermilk
- 2 tbsp vanilla extract
- 3 tbsp sugar
- 2 tsp red food Color
- 2-ounce chocolate chip
- 2 ⅓ tbsp whipped cream

Serving size: 4 crepes

Cooking time: 1 hour

Instructions

1. In a medium bowl, mix the flour with baking powder, baking soda, salt, and cocoa powder. Mix everything well. Set aside

2. In another bowl, add the buttermilk, egg, vanilla, sugar, red food coloring and whisk it.

3. Whisk it until it becomes smooth and fluffy.

4. Combine all these ingredients in another bowl. Mix well

5. Heat the non-stick pan over medium heat. Add 2 cups of batter on the pan and swirl properly to make it reach to the edge of the pan.

6. Cook until the color becomes brown.

7. Continue cooking from the other side.

8. Switch off the heat and put the crepes aside.

9. In a small bowl, beat the whipped cream, sugar and butter until it becomes smooth.

10. Add some chocolate chips to the mixture and whisk properly.

11. Start filling the crepes with this mixture. Add additional choco chips on the top of the crepe to garnish. Serve with hot chocolate drizzle.

12. Cinnamon Apple Crepe

Cinnamon gives the best crepe when combined with apples. Cinnamon crumbles crepe is a very simple yet delightful recipe enjoyed by everyone. Cinnamon is filled with many health benefits. The stuffed apples mixed with cinnamon and cream give the perfect taste to the crepe. While keeping your health prioritized, you can enjoy the crumble crepe anytime. The creamy sauce is prepared by a layer of buttercream and pinch of cinnamon.

Ingredients

- 4 apples finely chopped and washed
- 3 tbsp brown sugar
- 1 tsp cinnamon
- 2 cups all-purpose flour
- 1 cup buttermilk
- 1 cup milk
- ½ tsp salt
- 2 eggs
- 1 tbsp unsalted butter

Serving size: 4 crepes

Cooking time: 30 minutes

Instructions

1. In a big bowl, mix flour and salt together and mix it with your hands.

2. Add eggs in the same bowl. Mix egg and flour while pouring milk slowly in the bowl.

3. Whisk till the batter becomes smooth.

4. Leave it for 5-10 minutes.

5. Preheat the non-stick pan on medium-high flame.

6. Add ¼ of batter that is previously prepared on the pan and swirl it until the batter spreads properly all over the pan.

7. Let the edges cook properly. Flip around to cook it from the other side as well.

8. Continue cooking until the color of the crepe changes to brownish red.

9. Once cooked, transfer the crepe to a plate and keep it aside.

10. Add chopped apples in a bowl, add brown sugar and cinnamon. Mix everything well.

11. Let the apple leave its juice properly

12. Before serving, heat the apple mixture in low flame.

13. Fill the crepes with apple and cinnamon fillings.

14. To enhance the flavors, add Nutella or custard sauce on the top of the crepe and serve.

13. Nutella Strawberry Crepe

Nutella can never go wrong with any recipe. Although, you can create the best crepe using Nutella fillings. What else can be better than topping your crepe with strawberries? Well, you might suddenly start loving this extra chocolatey with extra berries crepe. The best part is that this crepe is effortless to make and requires common **Ingredients** like other crepes. Nutella with strawberries creates love. They are perfect for a midnight snack or even for your dinner table.

Ingredients

- 2 cups flour (all-purpose)
- 1 cup oat flour
- 2 tbsp brown sugar
- 2 eggs white
- 2 whole eggs
- 2 cups unsweetened almond milk
- 2 tbsp Nutella per crepe
- Juicy strawberries sliced
- Extra Nutella for garnishing

Serving size: 5 crepes

Cooking time: 40 minutes

Instructions

1. In a bowl, combine all crepe ingredients - flour, milk, eggs, brown sugar, oat flour, almond milk and whisk properly.

2. Whisk it until the batter becomes smooth and fluffy.

3. Preheat the pan and take 2 cups of batter and pour it on the pan.

4. Cook until it becomes brown in color.

5. Flip the crepe and continue cooking.

6. Once cooked properly, take the crepes off and keep aside.

7. Fill each crepe with Nutella and chopped strawberries.

8. Fold the crepe and again refill it.

9. Top with extra Nutella and whipped cream.

10. Serve with an extra layer of Nutella.

14. Brown butter Crepe with Bananas

How many of you love bananas? Well, they are slippery, of course, but when converted into a crepe, they taste delicious. Also, they are very healthy to consume. They are a good source for your breakfast table. Banana crepe and one glass of milk can do wonders in your breakfast routine, and you would be good to go. Brown butter gives a fluffy look to the batter, and hence, it tastes wonderful. For garnishing, you can use whipped cream or custard sauce.

Ingredients

- 1 cup all-purpose flour
- 2 cup flour
- 1 ½ tsp. salt
- 2 eggs
- 1 1/3 cup milk
- 5 tbsp. unsalted melted butter
- 2tbsp olive oil
- Nutella
- Bananas (4 pieces)

Serving size: 7 crepes

Cooking time: 40 minutes

Instructions

1. Firstly, melt the butter in a saucepan. Put 4 spoons of unsalted butter in a pan and mix smoothly.

2. Whisk for 2-3 minutes. After this, you will see brown bubbles coming from the surface of the pan.

3. Remove from the pan once the bubble occurs and whisk it for another 40 seconds.

4. In a medium bowl, mix the batter ingredients and whisk them properly.

5. Preheat the pan and add 3 cups of batter on it.

6. Swirl the pan to adjust the whole batter properly.

7. Cook until the color changes and then flip to the other side and continue cooking.

8. Mash bananas in a small bowl. Add Nutella, sugar and 2tbsp milk on it.

9. Whisk properly and fill the crepes with the banana filling.

10. Serve with extra Nutella spread.

15. Lemon Crepe

Lemon crepe has a delicious taste consisting of different sauces and lemon essence. They are refreshing and soothing. The lemon crepes are very thin and soft. They taste amazing when mixed with red wine. Unlike other crepes, the batter is made fluffy and thin. Lemon zest is fresh and energetic. It is good for digestion. It is best when taken as breakfast.

Ingredients

- 2 cups flour
- 1 ½ tsp. salt
- 2 eggs
- 1 1/3 cup milk
- 5 tbsp. unsalted melted butter
- 2tbsp olive oil
- 2tbsp vanilla extract
- Lemon caramel sauce
- Candied lemon slices

Serving size: 5 crepes

Cooking time: 45 minutes

Instructions

1. Add 3 tbsp of water to a pan and boil it. Add 6 tbsp of butter to the boiling water pan and let the butter melt.

2. In a medium bowl, whisk flour, salt, milk, sugar together.

3. Add vanilla and eggs to the mixture slowly.

4. Now, pour all of it in a butter mixture and whisk until the mixture becomes smooth.

5. Put the batter in an airtight container and refrigerate for 2 hours.

6. Preheat the oven to 200 degrees. Coat the non-stick skillet with butter.

7. Heat over medium flame till the smoke arises.

8. Add 3 tbsp of butter in the pan and swirl all around to spread the batter.

9. Cook until edges of crepe turn brown. Flip the crepe and cook from the other side as well.

10. Slide crepe onto an ovenproof plate; cover with foil, and transfer to the oven.

11. Fold the crepe in a triangle shape and pour the lemon caramel sauce and garnish with lemon zest slices.

16. Black Forest Crepe

The black forest crepe recipe involves fruity cherry toppings and caramel garnishing all over the crepe. Chocolate and cherry go side by side on every occasion. They are compatible with each other in terms of taste and texture. The black forest crepe is a specialty for late-night dinner in France.

Ingredients

- 2 cup flour
- 1 ½ tsp. salt
- 2 eggs
- 1 1/3 cup milk
- 3 tbsp. buttermilk
- 5 tbsp. unsalted melted butter
- 2 tbsp. olive oil
- 2 tbsp. sifted cocoa powder
- 3 cups of sugar
- 1-12 oz cherry pie filling
- 2 cups cool whipped cream
- 2 cup chocolate syrup

Serving size: 6 crepes

Cooking time: 50 minutes

Instructions

1. In a big bowl, mix flour and salt together and mix it with your hands.

2. Add eggs in the same bowl. Mix egg and flour while pouring milk slowly in the bowl.

3. Whisk till the batter becomes smooth.

4. Leave it for 5-10 minutes.

5. Preheat the non-stick pan in medium-high flame.

6. Add ¼ of batter that is previously prepared on the pan and swirl it until the batter spreads properly all over the pan.

7. Let the edges cook properly. Flip around to cook it from the other side as well.

8. Continue cooking until the color of the crepe changes to brownish red.

9. Once cooked, transfer the crepe to a plate and keep it aside.

10. In a bowl mix cherry pie fillings, the whipped cream, and sugar and keep it aside.

11. Whisk it until properly blended.

12. Fill the crepes with the cherry fillings and add caramel sauce on the top of the filling.

13. Top the crepes with chocolate sauce and enjoy!

17. Oreo Beer Crepe

Oreo is a famous cookie amongst kids these days. Well, adults are also kids when it comes to oreo! The oreo beer crepe is made from crispy oreo cookies and melted zest of beer. This is the best recipe to enjoy during your afternoon blooms. It tastes delicious. The amount of beer is almost negligible and hence, suitable for consumption by children. A mandatory crepe to try!

Ingredients

- 40g plain flour
- 120ml skimmed milk
- 1tsp vanilla extract
- 1tsp salt
- 2 eggs white
- ½ tbsp olive oil
- 6 oreo cookies
- Nutella
- Whipped cream

Serving size: 5 crepes

Cooking time: 30 minutes

Instructions

1. In a bowl, mix salt, flour, sugar, vanilla extract, milk, and egg whites.

2. Whisk the batter until it becomes smooth.

3. Once done, refrigerate the batter for 30 minutes.

4. In a small non-stick frying pan, pour 2-3 drops of olive oil.

5. Spoon 2 cups of batter in the pan and move the pan all around so that batter spreads properly.

6. Cook the batter until it turns brownish.

7. Flip the crepe and continue cooking.

8. In another bowl, mix vanilla extract, crumble oreo biscuits and Nutella. Whisk the mixture.

9. Fill the crepes with the oreo fillings one by one.

10. Serve with an extra layer of Nutella and whipped cream(optional) and enjoy!

18. Poppyseed Lemon Crepe with Blueberry Cream Filling

The name poppy seed is suggested from a flowering plant named poppy. Poppy flowers are elegant and colorful. As a result, their seeds are used for cooking various desserts and beverages. When lemon and poppy seeds are mixed, they taste scrumptious. And of course, blueberry, not to forget the best filling in the world for crepes. This amazing crepe recipe is ideal for breakfast and midday meals. Poppy Seed has many health benefits as well.

Ingredients

- 2 cup flour
- ½ tsp salt
- 3 tsp sugar
- 3 eggs
- 1 tsp. vanilla
- 2 cups of milk
- Zest of 1 ½ lemon
- 2tsp.poppyseed
- 1 tbsp. butter
- 2 tsp. Lemon juice

For blueberry cream fillings:

- 3 oz. Whipped cream
- ¼ cup of sugar powder
- ½ lemon zest
- 2tsp lemon juice
- 1 tsp. Vanilla
- 4 cups blueberry
- Nutella (garnishing)

Serving size: 6-8 crepes

Cooking time: 45 minutes

Instructions:

1. In a small pan, melt the butter.

2. In a small bowl, mix together flour, sugar, and salt and keep aside.

3. In another bowl, mix eggs white, milk, vanilla, lemon juice, lemon zest, and poppy seeds and whisk thoroughly.

4. Mix the wet mixture and dry mixture together properly.

5. Beat the mixture so that it does not form lumps.

6. Add melted butter to the mixture and whisk for 2-3 minutes.

7. In a separate bowl, pour whipped cream, sugar powder, lemon juice, lemon zest, and vanilla and mix it properly.

8. Add blueberries and smash them so that they get easily mixed in cream.

9. Whisk, whisk, and whisk.

10. Preheat the non-stick pan, add 1 cup of crepe batter on the pan and swirl the pan so that batter reaches the corner of the pan.

11. Cook until the color of the batter changes to brown-red.

12. Flip the crepe and cook from the other side as well.

13. Once cooked, keep them aside on a plate.

14. Fill each crepe with blueberry fillings properly.

15. Crepe is ready to serve. Add some Nutella on the top of the crepe. Enjoy!

19. Orange Crepe

Oranges have a high content of citric acid and a low-calorie fruit. It has a sweet taste with a little extra sour flavor. Oranges are used for making crepe fillings and orange sauce. They are famous for natural sweetness, which they add to the crepe. Orange crepes can fill your day with energy and freshness. Apart from this, an orange crepe is the best midday meal consumed by many people.

Ingredients

- 2 cup flour
- ½ tsp salt
- 3 tsp sugar
- 3 eggs
- 1 tsp. vanilla
- 2 cups of milk
- 2 cup of orange juice
- 1 tbsp. orange zest
- 1tsp cornstarch
- ½ tsp baking powder

Serving size: 4-5 crepes

Cooking time: 30 minutes

Instructions

1. In a small bowl, mix together flour, sugar, and salt and keep aside.

2. Add orange zest, orange juice, eggs, milk vanilla to the dry mixture.

3. Mix well until a smooth batter is formed.

4. Heat a pan and put ⅓ tsp of olive oil in it.

5. Pour 1 ½ cup of batter at the center of the pan.

6. Cook the batter properly until it's color becomes brownish.

7. Flip it to the other side and cook for 30 seconds.

8. Roll the crepe and put it on a plate.

9. In a separate bowl, mix 2 cup orange juice and 2tbsp of cornstarch. Stir.

10. Pour this mixture to a saucepan and stir till the sauce becomes thick and sticky.

11. Fill the crepes with the sauce and pour some of it on the top of the crepe.

12. Garnish it with whipped cream(optional).

13. Enjoy the crepe!

20. Mix Vegetable Crepe

The healthiest and savory food comes from the greatest idea of making mixed vegetables crepe. Mix vegetable crepe has deep traditional flavors of different vegetables together. A perfect lunch comes with varieties of veggies. This crepe recipe is very easy to prepare and totally healthy as well.

Ingredients

- 2 cups of cream
- 2 cup freshly chopped veggies, various types.
- 3 tbsp milk
- 2 tbsp lemon juice
- 1 tbsp salt
- 1 tbsp olive oil virgin
- 2 cups chopped zucchini
- 1 cup chopped green beans
- 1 cup fresh corn kernels
- ¼ tsp ground pepper
- 1 cup ricotta cheese

Serving size: 4-5 crepes

Cooking time: 40 minutes

Instructions

1. In a bowl, mix lemon juice, milk, ¼ tsp salt, sour cream. Whisk to combine.

2. Heat the skillet and pour olive oil. Add zucchini, green beans, and corn and cook.

3. Cook the veggies until they get brown in color.

4. Now, add ricotta, pepper, cheese and stir until color changes and cream melts.

5. Remove from the heat and keep aside.

6. Make the crepe batter. In a skillet, pour 2 cups of batter and swirl the skillet.

7. Cook the batter till the color changes to brown.

8. Flip the crepe and continue cooking.

9. Remove it from the pan and keep on a plate.

10. Add the vegetable fillings in each of the crepes separately.

11. Add parmesan cheese at the top of the crepe.

12. Serve with some corn kernels and lemon zest.

21. Chicken and Mushroom Crepe.

Chicken and mushroom crepe is a delicious choice to serve in a classy brunch and lunch as well. The best part about it is, the filling is soft and juicy, and it melts easily. It is surely not a traditional crepe recipe, but you cannot say no to a chicken and mushroom combination.

Ingredients

- 1 brown onion, chopped
- 250gms butter mushroom, sliced
- 200gms swiss mushroom, sliced
- 1 ½ tbsp thyme leaves
- 2 tsp olive oil
- 2 tbsp plain flour
- 250 ml cream for cooking
- 1 large barbecue chicken, chopped finely
- 2 packets of ready-made crepes
- Steamed vegetables
- 2 cups reduced-fat tasty cheese

Serving size: 5-6 crepes

Cooking time: 1 hour 30 minutes

Instructions

1. Preheat the non-stick frying pan at medium heat. Add onions and fry them.

2. Add mushrooms and thyme to it and cook for 10-15 minutes.

3. Add flour and stir until everything gets absorbed.

4. Add half of the heavy cream to the pan and stir.

5. After this add chicken to the mushroom gravy.

6. Cook for 15 minutes until the chicken gets thickened and soft.

7. Remove from heat and keep aside to cool.

8. Preheat the oven to 200°C fan-forced. Top the ready-made crepe with ¼ of the chicken fillings. Roll up and set aside.

9. Place 6 crepes in a 5 cm deep baking dish. Drizzle whipped cream over the crepes, seam side down.

10. Bake for 20 -25 minutes until golden.

11. Serve with pepper and BBQ sauce.

22. Apple Walnut Crepe

It's true when someone says, "an apple a day keeps doctors away." Well, yes! It seems true. Apples are the best remedy for all the problems. And walnuts! They add glory to the crepes. Apple walnut crepe is simple and easy to go recipe for all the health freaks out there. They are best for brunch and cheat days when you wish to eat something sweet.

Ingredients

- 1 ½ cup milk
- 2 cup flour
- 3 eggs
- 1 ½ tsp vanilla extract
- 2tbsp brown sugar
- 1 cup of water
- 1tbsp cinnamon
- 1tbsp cornstarch
- ¼ tsp nutmeg
- ½ chopped walnuts
- 4 chopped peeled apples

Serving size: 6 crepes

Cooking time: 30 minutes

Instructions

1. In a large bowl, whisk eggs, flour, milk and vanilla extract together.

2. Spray cooking oil on a skillet. Preheat it on low medium flame.

3. Pour 2 cups of batter on the skillet and swirl up to the corner.

4. Cook until the sides of the crepe are cooked properly.

5. Flip the crepe to the other side and continue cooking.

6. Remove the crepe from the pan and keep them aside.

7. Boil brown sugar and water in a saucepan. Mix cornstarch, nutmeg, and cinnamon together. Stir until the mixture becomes smooth.

8. Add chopped apples and walnut to the mixture and stir well.

9. Stir till the mixture becomes thick. Add cream and whisk.

10. Fill the crepes with this apple filling and serve. Enjoy!

23. Buckwheat Mushroom Savory Galette

Buckwheat and mushroom. They are some of the most flavorsome and comforting crepes for weekend lunch and daily breakfast. They are gluten-free and made with minimum oil. You can start your day with these amazing and tasty buckwheat mushroom crepes.

Ingredients

- 2 cups buckwheat flour
- ½ tsp salt
- 1tsp coconut sugar
- 2 tbsp ground flaxseed
- 2 cups almond milk.
- 1 onion (chopped)
- 30 oz mushrooms (chopped)
- 1 tsp cumin
- 1 ½ onion crushed
- 2 tbsp cornstarch
- 1 chopped kale

Serving size: 7-8 crepes

Cooking time: 40 minutes

Instructions

1. In a large bowl, mix buckwheat, flaxseed, coconut sugar, almond milk, and salt. Whisk the mixture.

2. Preheat a large nonstick skillet. Add 1 cup of batter to the pan and swirl properly.

3. Cook for 3 minutes and flip over. Continue cooking until the color changes to red-brown.

4. Remove the pan from heat and keep aside the crepe on a plate.

5. To a nonstick saucepan, add onion and cook for 2 minutes.

6. Add mushrooms and cook for 5-6 minutes properly.

7. After this add almond milk, cumin, cornstarch, salt, and kale. Cook for another 3 minutes until kale gets soft and the sauce becomes thick.

8. Fill the crepes with this filling and serve!

24. Shrimp Florentine Crepe

This meal is loved by most of the teenagers. It is a time taking recipe, but the results are ravishing. The juices of shrimp that melts in the crepe are delicious and considered perfect for a valentines dinner party. Apart from this, shrimp has many health benefits. Shrimp florentine is a must-try crepe. Not only does it taste delicious, but it also provides many surreal health benefits.

Ingredients

Crepe Ingredients

- 2 tbsp butter
- Mushrooms thin sliced
- 2 cup all-purpose flour
- 2 cup milk
- 2 tsp salt
- ¼ tsp pepper
- 12 oz frozen fresh shrimp
- 2 tbsp chopped fresh dill

Serving size: 6 crepes

Cooking time: 1 hour 20 minutes

Instructions

1. Heat the oven at 375°C. Spray 3-quart baking tray.

2. In a medium bowl, add eggs and flour and blend it until the mixture becomes smooth. Then add 1 cup milk and whisk.

3. Heat non-stick skillet. Lift the pan and add 2 cups of batter into it and swirl properly.

4. Turn the crepe and continue cooking. Cook until the crepe color changes to brownish red.

5. In another pan, pour butter and cook mushrooms in low medium flame. Once done, set them aside.

6. Now in another saucepan, melt 1 tbsp butter and add ⅓ cup flour and 2 cups of milk. Boil the mixture.

7. Add dill, salt, pepper, fresh shrimp and cooked mushrooms into it.

8. Cook for 5-6 minutes. Fill the crepes with this shrimp mixture.

9. Cover each crepe tightly and bake for 25 minutes.

10. Serve the crepes with whipped cream and mushrooms if desired.

25. Chocolate Strawberry Crepe

Chocolate crepe with a drizzle of strawberries is just heaven on the food plate. It is the best morning meal and brunch. The juices of strawberries combined with chocolate syrup are drizzling to the taste buds. It is easy to make this affordable dish. This crepe has all the goodness of chocolate and bright strawberries, which is extravagantly delicious in taste. They make the best morning breakfast.

Ingredients

- 2 cup flour
- ½ tsp salt
- 3 tsp sugar
- 3 eggs
- 1 tsp. vanilla
- 2 cups of milk
- 1 cup semisweet chocolate chips
- 1 ½ sliced strawberries
- Whipped cream

Serving size: 6 crepes

Cooking time: 30 minutes

Instructions

1. In a medium bowl, beat eggs, flour, milk, 1tsp vanilla, and salt and whisk until it becomes smooth.

2. Heat a nonstick skillet over the medium flame.

3. Pour 1 ½ cup of batter into the skillet and swirl to melt the edges.

4. Cook until the color of the crepe changes to brown. Flip the crepe and continue cooking.

5. Remove the crepes from the skillet and keep aside.

6. In a small saucepan, melt the chocolate chips.

7. Add sliced strawberries in the saucepan and stir. Add cream to the saucepan and stir till the sauce becomes thick and heavy.

8. Remove from the pan and fill the crepes with this chocolate strawberry sauce.

9. Garnish the crepe with sliced strawberries and whipped cream.

10. Serve. Enjoy!

26. Lemon Strawberry Crepe

Rich in vitamin C, Lemon Strawberry Crepes are delicious and comforting. You can easily prepare them at your home. They are easy to make and taste delicious. Zest of lemon mixed with the beautiful color of strawberry makes a perfect combination for the fillings. Since crepes are thin and soft, lemon zest can be added to provide a tempting taste to it.

Ingredients

- 2 cup flour
- ½ tsp salt
- 3 tsp sugar
- 3 eggs
- 1 tsp. vanilla
- 2 cups of milk
- 2 tbsp lemon juice
- 2tsp lemon zest
- 1 tbsp strawberry syrup

Serving size: 6-7 crepes

Cooking time: 30 minutes

Instructions

1. In a medium bowl, beat eggs, flour, milk, 1tsp vanilla and salt and lemon juice and strawberry syrup and whisk until it becomes smooth.

2. Heat a nonstick skillet over the medium flame.

3. Pour 1 ½ cup of batter into the skillet and swirl to melt the edges.

4. Cook until the color of crepe changes to brown. Flip the crepe and continue cooking.

5. Remove the crepes from the skillet and keep aside.

6. In another bowl, mix lemon juice, strawberry syrup, butter, sugar, cream and lemon zest.

7. Whisk it properly until the sauce becomes thick.

8. Fill the crepes with this sauce and keep aside for 10 minutes.

9. Serve with sliced lemon and strawberries.

10. If desired, top the crepes with whipped cream.

27. Vanilla Apple with Beer Crepe

Vanilla is as sweet as it looks. It has the essence of a ravishing aroma and delicious taste, which makes it perfect for the icing and filling process. Crepes are light and delicious when served with apples.

In France, beer crepes are consumed by most of the elders. Hence, making it the most demanded and popular crepe. Since beer has several health benefits, it is used for garnishing the entire crepe. A mixture of vanilla, beer, and apple is something unique to be considered.

Ingredients

- 1 vanilla pod
- 1 cup brown sugar
- 3 oz apples chopped
- Readymade crepe packet
- Whipped cream
- 1 tsp butter

Serving size: 7-8 crepes

Cooking time: 30 minutes

Instructions

1. Preheat the nonstick skillet and pour 1 tbsp butter on it.

2. Heat the crepe in the butter. Once done keep them aside in a plate.

3. Peel the apples and cut them into slices.

4. In a saucepan, boil the water and put 2 cups of chopped apples with ½ tsp lemon zest. Boil until the apples get soft.

5. After this, drain the excess juice or water from the saucepan.

6. Add sugar and seeds of split vanilla pod and simmer in low heat until everything cooks properly.

7. Fill this mixture in each crepe separately.

8. Serve with drizzled beer and whipped cream.

28. Lobster Newburg Crepe

They are rich in calcium and full of delicious sauces. This is perfect for lunch, dinner, brunch, or practically anytime. They taste heavenly and contain a smirking aroma of lobsters. Lobsters are rich in fatty acid contents. Hence, they are good for those who want to gain weight. They taste luscious when garnished with green beans and veggies. While lobsters are famous for their fluffy texture and tasty flesh, France is a big fan of lobster crepes. A must-try crepe for lunch.

Ingredients

- 4 cups lobster meat, cooked and chopped
- 2 cups whipping cream
- 7 tbsp butter
- 2 tbsp paprika
- 10 egg yolks
- 1 ½ dry sherry
- Salt
- 2 cups parmesan cheese
- Pepper

Serving size: 6 crepes

Cooking time: 40 minutes

Instructions

1. In a saucepan, melt the butter.

2. Add some cream and paprika and heat for 5 minutes

3. Add 2 egg yolks and whisk properly the whole mixture.

4. Add sherry to the mixture and cook properly.

5. Add lobster meat to the mixture, salt, and pepper, and stir.

6. Grease a small baking dish.

7. Fill the crepe with lobster mixture and sauce separately.

8. Roll the crepes and place them on a baking dish, seam side down.

9. Pour leftover sauce on top of the crepe and refrigerate.

10. While serving, preheat the crepes in a 350 degrees oven for 15 minutes and serve with cheese and cream.

29. Grape Cream Crepe

The juicy taste of red grapes is delicious. It looks wonderful at the plate. The color of the grape crepe is beautiful and bright. It is famous for its natural sweetness. You can easily prepare grape crepe in your kitchen with simple ingredients. Grapes are a great source of vitamin C. Hence, superfoods for people who need vitamin C in their daily routine. Dipped grapes in cream sauce are used for preparing the fillings of crepe.

Ingredients

- 4 cups lobster meat, cooked and chopped
- 2 cups whipping cream
- 7 tbsp butter
- 2 tbsp paprika
- 10 egg yolks
- 1 ½ dry sherry
- Salt
- 2 cups parmesan cheese
- Pepper

Serving size: 7-8 crepes

Cooking time: 30 minutes

Instructions

1. In a saucepan, melt the butter.

2. Add some cream and paprika and heat for 5 minutes.

3. Add 2 egg yolks and whisk properly the whole mixture.

4. Add sherry to the mixture and cook properly.

5. Add lobster meat to the mixture, salt, and pepper, and stir.

6. Grease a small baking dish.

7. Fill the crepe with lobster mixture and sauce separately.

8. Roll the crepes and place them on a baking dish, seam side down.

9. Pour leftover sauce on top of the crepe and refrigerate.

10. While serving, preheat the crepes in a 350 degrees oven for 15 minutes and serve with cheese and cream.

30. Avocado Crepe

Avocado crepes are usually consumed in the breakfast because of the nutrition it provides. It has lots of health benefits in day to day life. Avocado toast comes under a fat-burning diet. The crepe filling is prepared using avocado paste and cinnamon with lots of raw sugar. A must try crepe for summer beach parties. Various shakes and Avocado protein bars are produced from the essence of avocado.

Ingredients

- 2 cups wheat flour
- 2 eggs which are lightly beaten
- ¼ tsp salt
- 1 tsp olive oil
- 3 cups seedless red grapes
- 1tbsp cornstarch
- 2 cups of water
- 1 cup cream
- 1 tbsp sugar
- Nutella

Serving size: 6 crepes

Cooking time: 30 minutes

Instructions

1. Prepare the crepe batter. Whisk it properly.

2. In a nonstick skillet, pour the batter and swirl in low medium heat.

3. Flip the crepe and continue cooking until the color changes to brown.

4. In a saucepan, boil 1 cup water, butter, chopped avocado, and brown sugar to it.

5. Stir the mixture until it becomes a thick and heavy sauce.

6. Fold the crepes and fill them with avocado sauce.

7. Serve with Nutella drizzle and whipped cream(optional).

Conclusion

Well! With this, we come to the end of this amazing cookbook.

We hope you guys enjoyed it and have learned delicious crepe recipes that you can try at your kitchen. We hope you have discovered your inner talent while making these scrumptious desserts on your own.

Now, what's next?

Next, try every recipe in your kitchen and impress your family and friends. Once you master the art of making delicious crepes, try making your experimental recipes, and do let us know. Till then best of luck to you and enjoy the art of making crepes.

Good Luck, fellows!

About the Author

Ivy's mission is to share her recipes with the world. Even though she is not a professional cook she has always had that flair toward cooking. Her hands create magic. She can make even the simplest recipe tastes superb. Everyone who has tried her food has astounding their compliments was what made her think about writing recipes.

She wanted everyone to have a taste of her creations aside from close family and friends. So, deciding to write recipes was her winning decision. She isn't interested in popularity, but how many people have her recipes reached and touched people. Each recipe in her cookbooks is special and has a special meaning in her life. This means that each recipe is created with attention and love. Every ingredient carefully picked, every combination tried and tested.

Her mission started on her birthday about 9 years ago, when her guests couldn't stop prizing the food on the table. The next thing she did was organizing an event where chefs from restaurants were tasting her recipes. This event gave her the courage to start spreading her recipes.

She has written many cookbooks and she is still working on more. There is no end in the art of cooking; all you need is inspiration, love, and dedication.

Author's Afterthoughts

THANK YOU

I am thankful for downloading this book and taking the time to read it. I know that you have learned a lot and you had a great time reading it. Writing books is the best way to share the skills I have with your and the best tips too.

I know that there are many books and choosing my book is amazing. I am thankful that you stopped and took time to decide. You made a great decision and I am sure that you enjoyed it.

I will be even happier if you provide honest feedback about my book. Feedbacks helped by growing and they still do. They help me to choose better content and new ideas. So, maybe your feedback can trigger an idea for my next book.

Thank you again

Sincerely

Ivy Hope

Made in the USA
Coppell, TX
21 November 2020